FAMOUS NATIVE AMERICANS™

SITTING BULL:
Courageous Sioux Chief

Diane Shaughnessy

The Rosen Publishing Group's
PowerKids Press™
New York

Published in 1997 by The Rosen Publishing Group, Inc.
29 East 21st Street, New York, NY 10010

First Edition

Book Design: Danielle Primiceri

Photo Credits: Cover, pp. 8–9, 20 (both) © Archive Photos; pp. 4, 4–5 (background), 7, 12, 14–15 © Bettmann; pp. 11, 22 © Corbis-Bettmann; p. 16 © The Bettmann Archive; p. 19 AP/Wide World Photos.

Diane Shaughnessy
    Sitting Bull / Diane Shaughnessy.
        p.   cm. — (Famous Native Americans)
    Includes index.
    Summary: A biography of the Sioux chief who, although he led his people into the Battle of Little Big Horn, was also a man of mercy, wisdom, and peace.
    ISBN 0-8239-5109-X
    1. Sitting Bull, 1834?–1890—Juvenile literature. 2. Dakota Indians—Juvenile literature. 3. Hunkpapa Indians—Kings and rulers—Biography—Juvenile literature. 4. Hunkpapa Indians—History—Juvenile literature. [1. Sitting Bull, 1834?–1890. 2. Dakota Indians—Biography. 3. Hunkpapa Indians—Biography. 4. Indians of North America—Biography.] I. Title. II. Series.
    E99.D1S617 1997
    978'.004975'0092—dc21   97-220
                                                                                      CIP
                                                                                      AC

Manufactured in the United States of America

Contents

Sitting Bull

Sitting Bull was a brave **Sioux** (SOO) chief who fought to save his people's land and freedom. He was born in the early 1830s on the **plains** (PLAYNZ) of North America, in the area that is now South Dakota. He was named Hunkeshnee, a Sioux word that means "slow."

The Sioux were in what is now North Dakota and South Dakota. Sitting Bull's tribe traveled to Canada and lived there for four years. Then they returned to the plains.

Hunkeshnee thought about things very carefully before he did them.

The Sioux moved from place to place, hunting buffalo. Hunkeshnee belonged to the Hunkpapa, one of the many groups that made up the Sioux Indian **Nation** (NAY-shun).

◀ *Sitting Bull was a great Sioux chief who worked hard to save the freedom of his people and their land.*

5

Growing Up Sioux

Sioux boys learned important skills through the games they played. Hunkeshnee and the other boys hunted with bows and arrows, held races, wrestled, and swam. They also **imitated** (IM-ih-tay-ted) the way their fathers acted. Hunkeshnee proved to be a brave **warrior** (WAR-ee-yur) in play and in battle. He killed his first buffalo when he was ten. He won his first battle **honor** (ON-er) when he was fourteen. Hunkeshnee struck the first blow of the battle. After that, he was called Sitting Bull for his bravery and strength.

Hunkeshnee earned the name Sitting Bull by stopping a bull from charging at him. Hunkeshnee made the bull "sit."

The White People

Sitting Bull was named chief of the Hunkpapas during the 1860s. Around that time, gold was found on Sioux land in an area called the Black Hills. Many settlers from the east wanted to travel west to search for gold. The U.S. government sent soldiers to buy that land from the Sioux. But the Sioux did not want to sell it.

Chiefs Sitting Bull, Red Cloud, and Spotted Tail met with President Ulysses S. Grant to sign the Fort Laramie Treaty of 1868.

Sitting Bull wanted his people to be able to hunt and live freely on Sioux land. The U.S. government ordered the soldiers to fight for the land. Sitting Bull joined together with other Sioux chiefs and fought back. The soldiers offered the Sioux chiefs a peace **treaty** (TREE-tee), as long as the Sioux gave up some of their land. The Sioux wanted to stop the fighting, so they agreed.

9

To the Reservations

After the Sioux signed the treaty, soldiers tried to take more land. They forced the Sioux and other peoples to leave their own land and move to **reservations** (reh-zer-VAY-shunz). In 1876, Sitting Bull again joined with other Sioux chiefs to defend their land and freedom. During a gathering of the Sioux, Cheyenne, and Arapaho tribes, General George Custer attacked the Native Americans. Together, the tribes fought back and won their freedom for a few more years. This is known as the Battle of Little Big Horn.

Although many paintings of the Battle of Little Big Horn show General Custer winning the battle, it was really ▶ the Native Americans who won.

Moving On

After the battle, the different tribes went their own ways. Sitting Bull and the Sioux continued to hunt on what they thought of as their land. The treaty of 1868 said it was their land. But the government still wanted that land. Soldiers were sent to kill the buffalo that the Sioux hunted. The Sioux needed buffalo to **survive** (ser-VYV). They ate the meat, and made clothing and shelters from buffalo **hides** (HYDZ). The Sioux were tired of fighting, so they decided to leave. They moved north, to Canada.

It was a difficult decision for the Sioux to leave their home and move somewhere else.

13

Starvation

Sitting Bull and his people stayed in Canada for four years. But there were few buffalo left to hunt there. And the Sioux received little help from the Canadian government. The Sioux were once again without food or shelter.

Hungry, cold, and tired, they knew it was time to head to the Sioux reservation. Although this was exactly what the U.S. government wanted, the government was afraid Sitting Bull would try to fight again. Even though the government had promised not to, they put Sitting Bull in jail, where he stayed for two years.

Without buffalo to hunt, the Sioux were left hungry and cold. They returned home, only to move onto reservations.

The Wild West

By this time, Sitting Bull was **famous** (FAY-mus). A man named Buffalo Bill Cody visited Sitting Bull. He asked Sitting Bull to join his Wild West Show, which traveled around the country. Sitting Bull agreed. Americans couldn't wait to see him. They all wanted to meet the man who had defeated General Custer. When Buffalo Bill asked Sitting Bull to travel to England with the show, Sitting Bull said no. He returned home, where he and his people lived peacefully, farming and raising horses and cattle.

Sitting Bull learned a lot about the white people when he traveled with Buffalo Bill's Wild West Show.

A Sign of Hope

Soon after Sitting Bull returned to his people, members of the government decided that they wanted more land from the Sioux reservation. Sitting Bull **refused** (ree-FYOOZD) to give it up. But other Sioux chiefs later sold most of it to the government. Sitting Bull saw how sad and hurt his people were. He wanted to give them hope that things would get better. He allowed his people to do the ghost dance. The ghost dance was a way of praying, and praying was an important part of Sioux life. Prayer led to hope.

Dancing is very important to the Sioux. It is a way to pray and to gather strength. Here a group prepares for a "Battle Dance." ▶

Fighting Until the End

The government was afraid that the ghost dance would give the Sioux enough hope and strength to fight back. The Sioux were ordered to give up the right to do the dance, but they refused. So the government decided to **arrest** (uh-REST) Sitting Bull to keep the Sioux quiet. When Sioux soldiers, who worked for the government, arrived to take him away, Sitting Bull's brother tried to **protect** (pro-TEKT) him. The brother fired a shot by mistake. The soldiers fired back, killing Sitting Bull, his brother, his son, and twelve other people.

◀ *This man is believed to be the soldier who shot the great chief, Sitting Bull.*

Strength and Courage

Sitting Bull was a man of great strength and **courage** (KER-ej). He wanted only the best for his people. He once said, "The Great Spirit gave us this land, and we are at home here." He fought hard for what he believed in—the freedom for his people to live in peace on their land.

Sitting Bull's strength inspired his people to fight hard for their land and freedom.